A TRUE BOOK™

THE EARTH AT RISK

TUNDRA IN DANGER

Natasha Vizcarra

Children's Press®
An imprint of Scholastic Inc.

Content Consultant
Matthew Sturm, Ph.D.
University of Alaska Fairbanks

Library of Congress Cataloging-in-Publication Data available
ISBN 978-1-5461-0215-1 (library binding) | ISBN 978-1-5461-0216-8 (paperback) |
ISBN 978-1-5461-0217-5 (ebook)

10 9 8 7 6 5 4 3 2 1   •   25 26 27 28 29

Printed in China 62
First edition, 2025

Design by Kathleen Petelinsek
Series produced by Spooky Cheetah Press

Front cover: The tundra faces many threats, including rising global temperatures, drilling, and wildfires.

Find the Truth!

Everything you are about to read is true *except* for one of the sentences on this page.

Which one is **TRUE**?

T or F Most tundra is found in protected lands.

T or F Ancient viruses in the tundra can be revived.

Find the answers in this book.

What's in This Book?

The **BIG** Truth

Animals on the Move

Snow leopards live
in alpine tundra
across Asia.

This bumblebee is able to survive in the freezing Arctic tundra.

Caribou have adapted to live in the Arctic tundra.

The tundra is one of Earth's coldest and harshest **biomes**. It can be **covered in snow** for up to nine months of the year. The tundra doesn't receive much **precipitation**. Each year, just 6 to 10 inches (15.2 to 25.4 centimeters) of **rain or snow** fall.

Tundra comes from the Finnish word *tunturia*. It means "treeless plain."

Only the **hardiest plants and animals** can survive here. Today, the tundra is at risk due to human activities, especially those that contribute to **climate change**. Some of the animals that live here are also at risk of becoming **endangered**. Luckily, people are working to save these wild places.

Caribou live in large herds in the Arctic tundra. Every year they shed their antlers and grow a new pair.

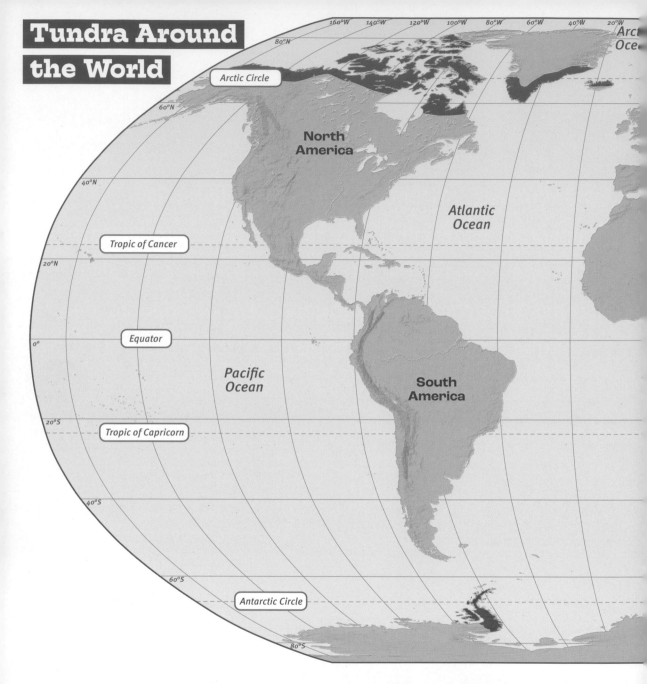

Arctic Ocean

80°N

Arctic Circle

60°N

North America

40°N

Atlantic Ocean

Tropic of Cancer

20°N

Equator

0°

Pacific Ocean

South America

20°S

Tropic of Capricorn

40°S

60°S

Antarctic Circle

80°S

160°W 140°W 120°W 100°W 80°W 60°W 40°W 20°W

There are two **types of tundra**. **Arctic tundra** is found near the Arctic Circle. It is also found on the Antarctic peninsula.

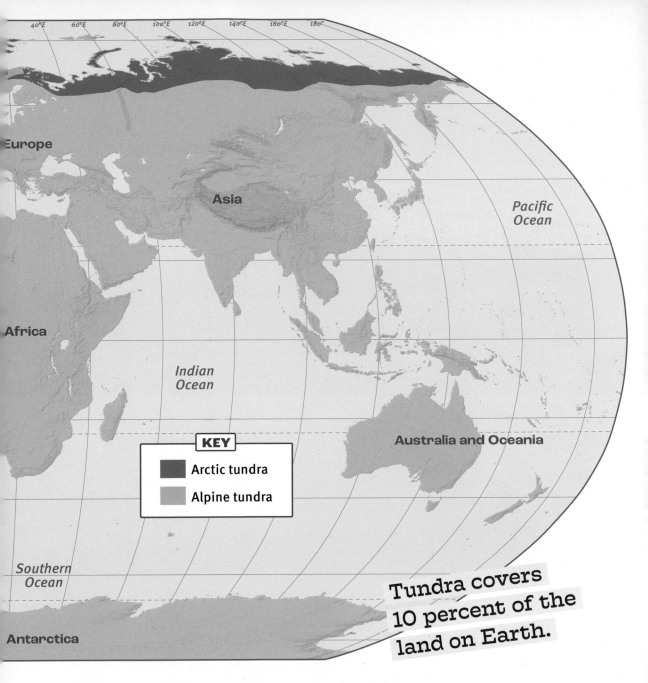

40°E 60°E 80°E 100°E 120°E 140°E 160°E 180°

Europe

Asia

Pacific
Ocean

Africa

Indian
Ocean

Australia and Oceania

KEY
- Arctic tundra
- Alpine tundra

Southern
Ocean

Tundra covers
10 percent of the
land on Earth.

Antarctica

Alpine tundra is found in high-**altitude**
regions—on mountaintops around the world.

In some parts of the Arctic tundra, the sun doesn't rise for two months during winter.

winter

The sun never sets during the Arctic summer.

summer

These photos show the Arctic tundra in winter (top) and summer (bottom).

The Frigid Far Reaches

In the Arctic, the tundra has two seasons. Winter typically lasts from September to June when the temperature can go as low as −80 degrees Fahrenheit (−62 degrees Celsius). Summer is short—just July and August. Summer temperatures can reach 54°F (12°C). Plant and animal species that live in the tundra are uniquely adapted to these conditions. In fact, some animals that live there cannot live anyplace else on Earth.

Permanently Frozen Ground

The Arctic tundra is a snowy landscape in winter. In summer, the rolling ground is covered in patches of rocks, low plants, and standing water. Strong winds, blowing snow, and low temperatures keep tundra plants from growing tall. They cannot have deep roots either. Sunlight thaws up to only about the top 20 in. (50.8 cm) of soil. Below that is permanently frozen ground called permafrost. Permafrost is ground that has been frozen for at least two years.

Because the ground is frozen, any rain or snow that falls in the Arctic tundra creates ponds and puddles rather than soaking into the ground.

This photo shows the layer of permafrost beneath the soil in the tundra.

reindeer lichen

tall cotton grass

Arctic willow is a shrub.

Arctic moss

The oldest reported Arctic willow was 236 years old. It was found in East Greenland.

Short, Hardy Plants

Lichens, mosses, grasses, low shrubs, and sedges cover the ground in the Arctic tundra year-round. Lichens are plantlike structures. They have no roots, stems, or leaves. Like mosses, they grow very low to the ground. Tundra grasses and sedges, which are grasslike plants, grow a bit taller. Shrubs produce about 50 kinds of wild berries—a source of food for Arctic wildlife and people. The plants don't die in winter. They just go **dormant**. They won't grow again until summer.

13

Keeping Toasty

Animals in the Arctic tundra have different ways of staying warm. Arctic foxes and hares have thick fur. Musk oxen and caribou have two layers of fur. Polar bears have two layers of fur and thick body fat. They also have small ears compared to other bears. That helps keep their body heat from escaping into the air around them.

Arctic fox

Arctic hare

musk ox

polar bear

Some animals—like Arctic foxes and Arctic hares—have white fur only in winter. That helps them blend into their snowy surroundings.

Faraway Food

In winter, some animals travel great distances to find food. Caribou move around the tundra searching for the thinnest snow. They push the crust of the snow downward. Then they paw it away and feed on the plants below. Most bird species leave the tundra to find food. Greater snow geese, Arctic loons, and snow buntings all **migrate**—in search of warmer weather—when summer ends.

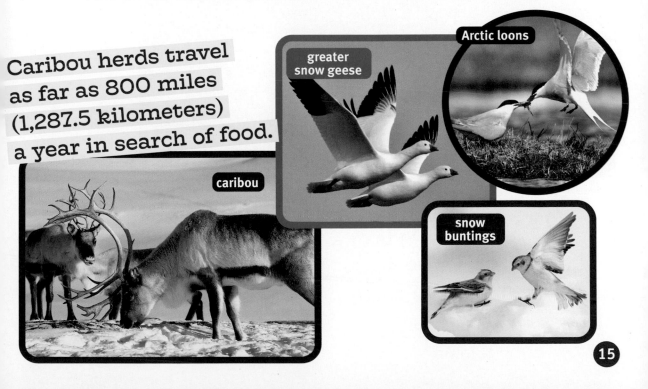

Caribou herds travel as far as 800 miles (1,287.5 kilometers) a year in search of food.

Arctic loons

greater snow geese

caribou

snow buntings

A Long Snooze

Some animals **hibernate** to survive winter. Arctic ground squirrels sleep in burrows under the snow. Arctic bumblebees slumber in underground burrows. Wood frogs freeze in the ground. During hibernation, the animals don't eat, and their breathing and heartbeat slow down.

Arctic ground squirrel

Arctic bumblebee

The wood frog is one animal whose heart stops beating during hibernation.

wood frog

Home on the Tundra

Yup'ik person

Sámi people

Hundreds of thousands of **Indigenous peoples** from more than 40 different groups live in the Arctic tundra. For example, the Yup'ik people live in the Alaskan tundra. The Sámi people live in Sápmi—an area that stretches across the northern parts of Finland, Norway, Russia, and Sweden. The Nenet people live in the northernmost reaches of Russia. To live comfortably in the cold, some Arctic peoples wear traditional furry parkas and boots made of caribou hide. Some travel by snowmobile or dog sled. Some communities herd reindeer for a living.

Nenet person

Caribou that are raised by people are often called reindeer.

Animals on the Move

There are three species of bears in North America: black bears, grizzly bears, and polar bears. They usually live in different habitats. But this changed in 2011, when scientists first observed all of them at the same time in Wapusk National Park at the edge of the Canadian tundra. Experts say this change in behavior is a result of global warming—the gradual rise in the temperature of Earth's atmosphere, caused by human activities that pollute. Here's what they think is happening.

Climate change includes global warming as well as other changes in the weather and weather patterns that are happening because of human activity.

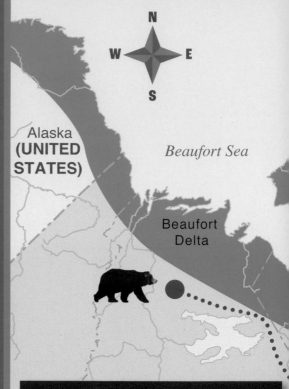

Alaska **(UNITED STATES)**

Beaufort Sea

Beaufort Delta

Black Bears

Black bears live in forested areas. The individuals that have been spotted in Wapusk usually live in the forest that lies just south and west of the park. Among other things, the warming climate has changed the availability of plants that black bears like to eat. Plants are growing farther north than they used to. And they are growing earlier in the season. Black bears are entering Wapusk in search of food.

Grizzly Bears

Grizzly bears are mostly found in woodland, forest, meadow, and prairie habitats. Experts think the grizzlies seen at Wapusk are from the Beaufort Delta, which is northwest of the park. Like black bears, grizzlies are facing a change in resources. They have had to expand their range—in many directions—in order to find food.

Polar Bears

Polar bears live in the tundra and have always been found at Wapusk for part of the year. In winter, they hunt on the sea ice in Hudson Bay. When the ice melts, the bears come ashore to feed. Global warming is causing sea ice to melt earlier in the season and to refreeze later, so the polar bears are spending more time in the park.

Hudson Bay

Wapusk
National Park

CANADA

Many plants in the Andean tundra are unique to that part of the world.

Alpine tundra is found in the Andes mountain range in South America.

On Mountain Peaks

Alpine tundra is found in high-altitude regions worldwide. Those include regions near the equator, because it is always cold on high mountaintops. Summers in the alpine tundra range from 37°F to 54°F (3°C to 12°C). Winters usually average 0°F (−18°C), but it is still too cold, dry, and windy for trees to grow here. Instead, you will find boulder fields, meadows with low-growing plants, and steep slopes covered in loose rocks and boulders.

Low and Fuzzy

Alpine tundra plants have to protect themselves against strong winds, low temperatures, blowing snow, and harsh sunlight. Spreading phlox and white mountain avens spread across the ground rather than growing upward. Pasqueflowers and woolly pussytoes grow dense hairs on their stems and leaves. Like a winter coat, the fuzzy hairs block the wind and hold in heat.

spreading phlox

white mountain avens

pasqueflowers

woolly pussytoes

The largest area of alpine tundra is found on the Tibetan Plateau in Asia.

glory-of-the-snow

purple mountain saxifrage

moss campion

Hiders and Huddlers

Other plants, like glory-of-the-snow, form flower buds beneath the winter snow. The ground is warmer there, and the snow acts as insulation. When the snow melts in summer, the flowers are ready to unfurl. Many plants, like purple mountain saxifrage and moss campion, grow huddled together to conserve heat and moisture.

Surviving the Winter

Some animals live in the alpine tundra year-round. Many, like the American pika, the Himalayan tahr, and the chinchilla of South America, have thick fur to keep them warm. Other animals, like the yellow-bellied marmot in North America, eat as much vegetation as they can in summer and early fall. Then they hibernate in winter.

American pika

Himalayan tahr

chinchilla

yellow-bellied marmot

A chinchilla's fur is so thick, as many as 60 hairs grow from a single hair follicle or root.

golden eagle

white-tailed ptarmigan in summer

white-tailed ptarmigan in winter

Avoiding Hunters

Adjusting with the seasons is not just about surviving the cold. Some alpine animals hide from hunters, like the golden eagle, by changing their colors to blend in with their surroundings. For example, the white-tailed ptarmigan is covered in speckled brown feathers in summer. In winter, it grows white feathers to blend in with the snow.

Part-Time Mountaineers

Many animals live in the alpine tundra for just part of the year. Bighorn sheep in North America and alpine ibex in Europe feed on the lush tundra plants in summer. In winter, they head to lower altitudes to find food. The snow leopard, a **predator** in Asia, roams across vast distances too.

bighorn sheep

alpine ibex

snow leopard

Wild yaks live on the Tibetan Plateau in Asia year-round.

Like humans, land animals need oxygen to survive.

Built for Thinner Air

Animals in the alpine tundra face a unique problem. There is less oxygen at high altitudes. They have adapted to this in different ways. For example, the wild yak has large lungs to take in a lot of air. It also has more hemoglobin than other animals. That is the molecule that carries oxygen in the blood. Finally, the yak has a large heart that moves the oxygen-rich blood through its body efficiently.

The Arctic is heating 2.5 times faster than the rest of the planet.

Permafrost on the Yukon Delta in Alaska is thawing.

Tundra Under Threat

Scientists predict that only 30 percent of the Siberian tundra will remain by 2050. Other studies say it will vanish entirely. If that happens, the animals that live in this tundra may vanish too. The tundra is disappearing largely because of destructive human activities. Many people are now working on ways to save this important biome.

The oldest permafrost is 740,000 years old. It is found in Yukon, Canada.

A giant sinkhole on the Yamal Peninsula, Siberia

Permanent No More

Rising temperatures in the Arctic tundra cause permafrost to thaw. When that happens, soil above the permafrost can slump, creating holes in the ground. Thawing permafrost has caused close to 20 giant sinkholes in Siberia. Some can be around 66 feet (20 meters) wide and 171 ft. (52 m) deep! Hundreds of tundra ponds in West Greenland have drained into thawing permafrost.

Defrosted Dangers

In 2014, a French scientist revived a virus that had been frozen in Siberian permafrost for 30,000 years. Other scientists have revived ancient bacteria and fungi. As the tundra's frozen layer thaws, more ancient **microbes** could wake up. In the past, companies buried toxic pollutants and radioactive waste in Arctic permafrost. Thawing permafrost could expose these dangerous materials too.

A scientist digs into thawing permafrost.

The tiny wormlike *Bdelloid rotifer* can wriggle back to life after being frozen in the Siberian tundra for 24,000 years.

The Greening of the Arctic

Rising temperatures are causing normally short tundra shrubs to grow taller. They are also causing trees to grow in the southern edges of the tundra. In 2009, scientists estimated that the Arctic tree line could creep 310 mi. (500 km) northward by 2100. If that happens, about half of the Arctic tundra from Siberia to Canada will disappear.

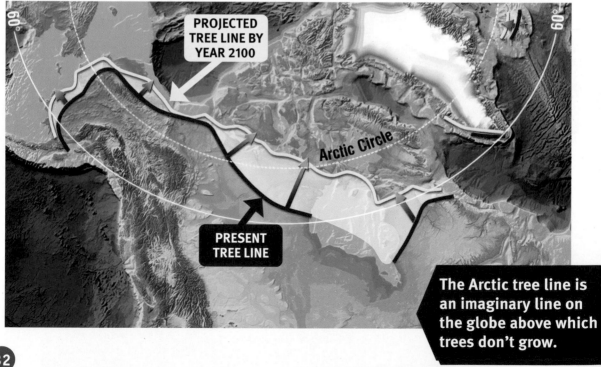

PROJECTED TREE LINE BY YEAR 2100

Arctic Circle

PRESENT TREE LINE

The Arctic tree line is an imaginary line on the globe above which trees don't grow.

A 2007 lightning-strike fire in Alaska's tundra burned for nearly three months.

Fire from the Sky

Tundra wildfires have become more common over the last two decades. This is also happening because of rising temperatures. Warmer weather dries out the plants in summer. And warmer air holds more moisture than is usually found in this region. That boosts the chances of lightning strikes occurring. When lightning hits dry plants, fire often follows.

A snowy owl swoops low to capture its prey.

Dangerous Rain

Climate change increases rain in the Arctic tundra. When rainwater freezes on the snowy surface, it forms thick ice crusts. The ice layers prevent caribou from feeding, causing many to starve. The icy crust harms lemmings, voles, and birds that shelter in the snow. Snowy owls and Arctic foxes that feed on lemmings are also affected.

A Fragile Habitat

Industries that mine minerals, oil, and gas also cause damage to the tundra. Tire tracks from heavy vehicles and chemical spills damage soil and plants. It takes a long time for these to recover. That means less food for tundra animals.

Caribou depend on low-growing lichen in the Arctic winters.

This structure is used to drill an oil and gas well in the Arctic tundra.

Why Protect the Tundra?

Protecting the tundra protects all of us from a warming climate. Permafrost under the Arctic tundra stores a huge amount of carbon. When permafrost thaws, this carbon is released into the atmosphere, turning up the heat on the rest of the planet even more.

Permafrost carbon is made of remnants of microbes, plants, and animals that lived and died in the tundra long ago.

A Yup'ik elder stands at the edge of land that is being washed away as the permafrost thaws.

The Arctic National Wildlife Refuge in Alaska is located on the traditional homelands of the Iñupiat and Gwich'in Peoples.

Safe Places Up North

A refuge is a protected place where threatened animal species are kept safe from hunting or changes to the environment like those caused by the mining industry. Creating more of these sanctuaries in the Arctic tundra can save species that are sensitive to rising temperatures. About 20 percent of Arctic tundra is already located in refuges. Scientists say we need more.

Phasing Out Fossil Fuels

Banning oil drilling protects the tundra from damage and pollution. And reducing our use of those fossil fuels lowers **greenhouse gas** emissions and can help stop global warming. The United States canceled oil and gas drilling in the Arctic National Wildlife Refuge, and Greenland has banned oil drilling in the whole country. Denmark and Costa Rica will stop drilling by 2050.

Timeline: Tundra in Danger

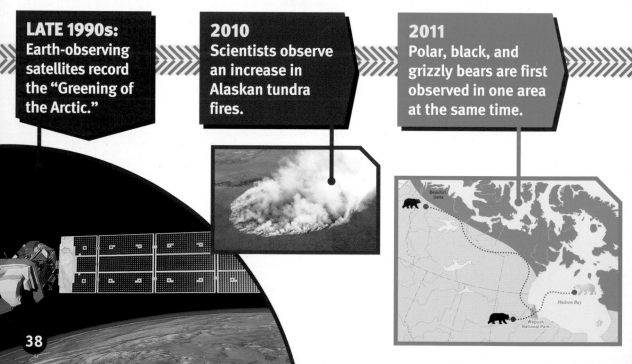

LATE 1990s: Earth-observing satellites record the "Greening of the Arctic."

2010 Scientists observe an increase in Alaskan tundra fires.

2011 Polar, black, and grizzly bears are first observed in one area at the same time.

Beaufort Delta

Hudson Bay

Wapusk National Park

The Tundra's Best Chance

To protect the tundra and the animals that live there, we need to stop climate change. Almost 200 countries have pledged to do so in the Paris Agreement. Many are shifting to cleaner forms of energy, like solar and wind. The cooperation of governments—and citizens—around the world is one important key to saving this incredible biome.

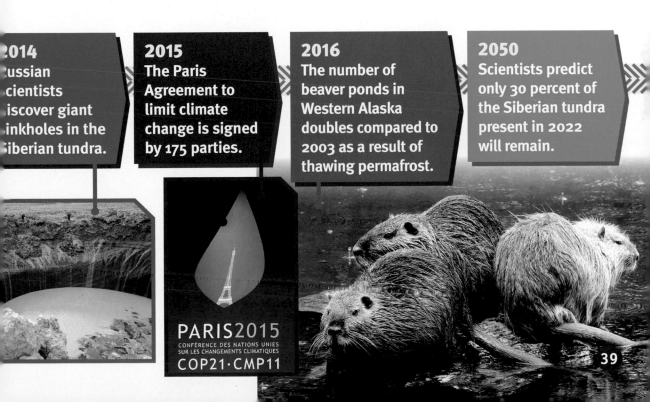

2014
Russian scientists discover giant sinkholes in the Siberian tundra.

2015
The Paris Agreement to limit climate change is signed by 175 parties.

2016
The number of beaver ponds in Western Alaska doubles compared to 2003 as a result of thawing permafrost.

2050
Scientists predict only 30 percent of the Siberian tundra present in 2022 will remain.

PARIS2015
CONFÉRENCE DES NATIONS UNIES
SUR LES CHANGEMENTS CLIMATIQUES
COP21·CMP11

Amazing Comeback

Musk oxen used to be found in Alaska, Canada, and Greenland. Then, in 1900, these shaggy-haired animals became extinct in Alaska. A change in climate and overhunting wiped them out. All hope was not lost, though, because wild musk oxen still existed in Greenland and Canada.

The musk oxen in Fairbanks that helped repopulate Alaska

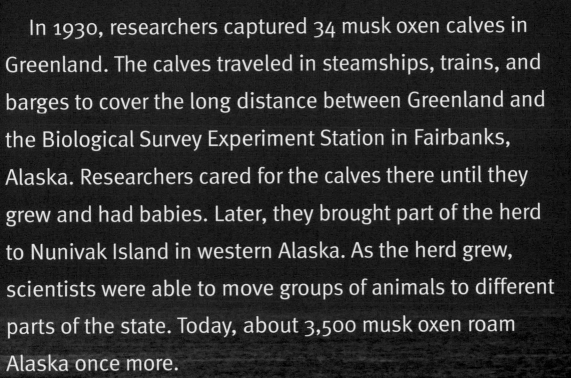

In 1930, researchers captured 34 musk oxen calves in Greenland. The calves traveled in steamships, trains, and barges to cover the long distance between Greenland and the Biological Survey Experiment Station in Fairbanks, Alaska. Researchers cared for the calves there until they grew and had babies. Later, they brought part of the herd to Nunivak Island in western Alaska. As the herd grew, scientists were able to move groups of animals to different parts of the state. Today, about 3,500 musk oxen roam Alaska once more.

Kid Heroes

Iluuna Sørensen is a climate activist who grew up on Greenland's tundra. She is part of the Arctic Angels. This group of more than 50 young women urges governments around the world to reduce fossil fuel emissions to save the Arctic ecosystem. Read this interview to learn more about Sørensen and her work.

1

Q: What's it like to grow up in the tundra?

A: In summer, we have 24 hours of daylight. That was hard to understand when I was a kid. Why go to bed when the sun is still out? Sometimes you can see the sunset and the sunrise in one hour.

2

Q: How did you learn about climate change?

A: I was nine when I watched a documentary on climate change. I didn't know what to do or what to say. I felt that maybe grown-ups can fix climate change.

3

Q: What motivated you to act on climate change?

A: In 2019, I joined marches to stop climate change. We got off school. We marched in Nuuk (the capital of Greenland). It was cool that we could talk to politicians. The politicians said that focusing on climate change should be a priority.

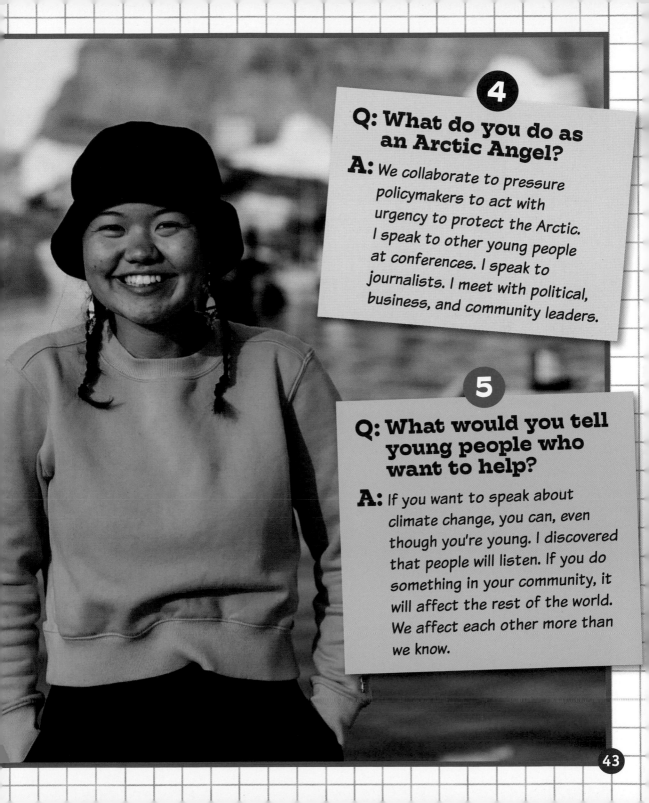

4

Q: What do you do as an Arctic Angel?

A: We collaborate to pressure policymakers to act with urgency to protect the Arctic. I speak to other young people at conferences. I speak to journalists. I meet with political, business, and community leaders.

5

Q: What would you tell young people who want to help?

A: If you want to speak about climate change, you can, even though you're young. I discovered that people will listen. If you do something in your community, it will affect the rest of the world. We affect each other more than we know.

43

True Statistics*

Percent of Earth's land surface that is covered by tundra: 10%

Average winter temperature in the Arctic tundra: −30°F/−34°C

Inches of rain Arctic tundra receives yearly: 6 to 10

Projected percent increase of precipitation in Arctic tundra by 2100: 30 to 60%

Number of tons of carbon stored in Arctic tundra: 1.9 trillion

Average winter temperature in alpine tundra: 0°F/−18°C

Inches of rain alpine tundra receives yearly: 6 to 10

Projected percent increase in plant height in the tundra by 2100: 20 to 60%

As of 2024

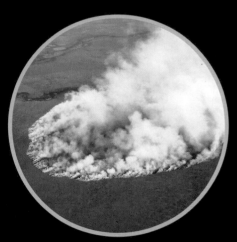

Did you find the truth?

F Most tundra is found in protected lands.

T Ancient viruses in the tundra can be revived.

Resources

Other books in this series:

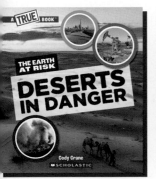   

You can also look at:

Bow, James. *Tundras Inside Out*. New York: Crabtree Publishing, 2015.

Gray, Susan Heinrichs. *Tundra*. Minneapolis, MN: Compass Point Books, 2001.

Johnson, Rebecca L. *A Walk in the Tundra*. New York: Lerner Publications, 2021.

Simpson, Phillip W. *Tundra Biomes Around the World*. Minneapolis, MN: Capstone Press, 2019.

Glossary

altitude (AL-ti-tood) the height of something above the ground or above sea level

biomes (BYE-ohmz) regions of the world with similar animals and plants

climate change (KLYE-mit CHAYNJ) global warming and other changes in the weather and weather patterns that are happening because of human activity

dormant (DOR-muhnt) a plant or seed that is alive but not growing

endangered (en-DAYN-jurd) in danger of becoming extinct, usually because of human activity

greenhouse gas (GREEN-hous GAS) a gas that traps heat in Earth's atmosphere

hibernate (HYE-bur-nate) to spend the winter in a sleeping or resting state

Indigenous peoples (in-DI-juh-nuhs PEE-puhlz) the first known inhabitants of a place

microbes (MYE-krohbz) extremely small living things, especially those that cause disease

migrate (MYE-grate) to move to another area or climate at a particular time of year

predator (PRED-uh-tur) an animal that lives by hunting other animals for food

Index

Page numbers in **bold** indicate illustrations.

About the Author

Natasha Vizcarra is a science writer and children's book author. She worked for many years with scientists who study frozen regions of the Earth. She has also lived in snowy Minnesota. That's enough snow and ice for her! She now lives in sunny Colorado with her husband, Chris, and their cats, Rico, Pepe, and Krakee the Kraken. Read more about Natasha's writing at www.natashavizcarra.com.